Saving the

The CHOCOLATE PILOT

Dona Herweck Rice

Consultant

Jessica White and her students
Pride Elementary School
Hillsborough County Public Schools

Publishing Credits

Rachelle Cracchiolo, M.S.Ed., *Publisher*

Conni Medina, M.A.Ed., *Editor in Chief*

Emily R. Smith, M.A.Ed., *Content Director*

Véronique Bos, *Creative Director*

Robin Erickson, *Art Director*

Michelle Jovin, M.A., *Associate Editor*

Lee Aucoin, *Senior Graphic Designer*

Teacher Created Materials would like to thank Chavi Lakhotia for suggesting the idea for this book.

Image Credits:
front cover (top), back cover, p.1, p.4 (top), p.17 (top), p.18 (bottom), p.19, p.24, p.25, p.26 (top, bottom), p.31, p.32 Courtesy Gail Halvorsen; front cover (bottom), p.1 U.S. Air Force; pp.2–3 akg-images/Newscom; p.5 The LIFE Picture Collection/Getty Images; p.6 Library of Congress [LC-USF34-037392-D]; p.7 (top) Library of Congress [LC-USZ62-115128]; p.7 (bottom) Library of Congress [LC-DIG-ppmsca-31771]; p.8 U.S. Navy; p.10 (background) Imperial War Museum [C 5284]; p.12 National Numismatic Collection, National Museum of American History; p.13, p.29 Associated Press; p.14 Imperial War Museum [MH 30687]; p.15 U.S. National Archives; p.16, p.23 (top) Bettmann Archive/Getty Images; p.17 (bottom) The Advertising Archives/Alamy; p.18 (top) Hulton Deutsch/Getty Images; pp.18–19 (background) Horst Sturm/picture-alliance/ZB/Newscom; p.18 (background) picture-alliance/ZB/Newscom; p.20 PjrStudio/Alamy; p.21 U.S. Department of Defense; p.22 dpa/picture-alliance/dpa/AP Images; p.23 (bottom) The Salt Lake Tribune [15 October 1949, page 3]; pp.26–27 (background) History Office, Air Mobility Command, Scott Air Force Base; p.27 Norbert Klähn/Wikimedia; p.28 (middle) Ralph Orlowski/Getty Images; p.28 (bottom) SchulteProductions/iStock; all other images from iStock and/or Shutterstock.

Library of Congress Cataloging-in-Publication Data

Names: Rice, Dona, author.
Title: The Chocolate Pilot / Dona Herweck Rice.
Description: Huntington Beach, CA : Teacher Created Materials, 2019. | Includes bibliographical references and index. | Audience: K-Grade 3.
Identifiers: LCCN 2019006964 | ISBN 9781644910047 (pbk. : alk. paper)
Subjects: LCSH: Berlin (Germany)--History--Blockade, 1948-1949--Juvenile literature. | Halvorsen, Gail S.--Juvenile literature. | United States. Air Force. Military Airlift Command--Biography--Juvenile literature. | Air pilots, Military--United States--Biography--Juvenile literature. | CYAC: Berlin (Germany)--History--Blockade, 1948-1949.
Classification: LCC DD881 .R486 2019 | DDC 943/.1550874092 [B]
--dc23 LC record available at https://lccn.loc.gov/2019006964

Teacher Created Materials

5301 Oceanus Drive
Huntington Beach, CA 92649-1030
www.tcmpub.com
ISBN 978-1-6449-1004-7

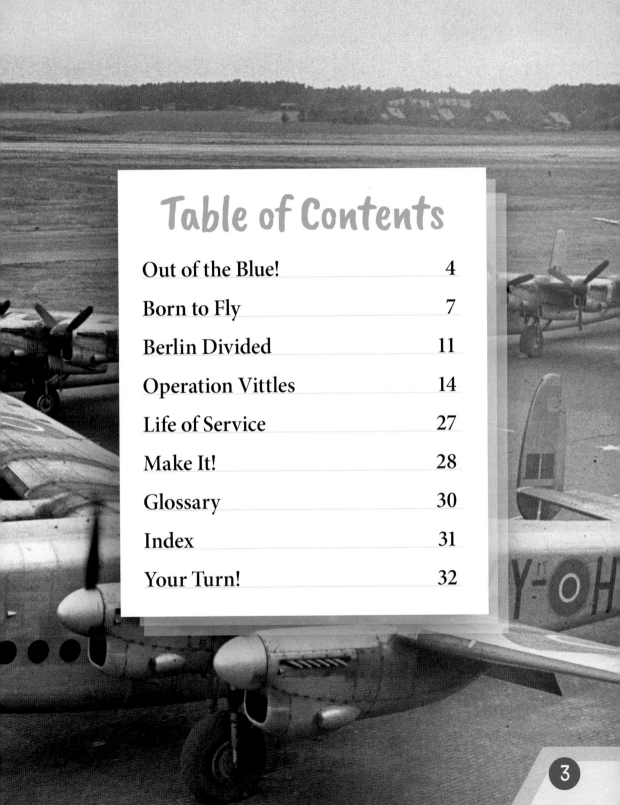

Table of Contents

Out of the Blue!

Overhead, in the bright blue sky, a plane flew closer and closer. It rolled back and forth before opening a hatch. Three small parachutes **wafted** to the ground. *Plop, plop, plop.* They landed at the feet of 30 children waiting beyond the barbed wire fence, just as they had been directed to do. They knew the parachutes were coming. Uncle Wiggly Wings had promised them.

As he had also promised, there was a treasure tied to every parachute. It was chocolate and gum. Sweets from the sky dropped at their feet. The children barely had food to eat. Sweet treats were beyond imagining! As Uncle Wiggly Wings—the Chocolate Pilot—flew away, the children waved the parachutes into the air. "Thank you, Uncle!" they seemed to say.

History of Chocolate

The first chocolate dates back more than 3,000 years. But chocolate remained rare until the end of the nineteenth century. That is when a Dutch man made a chocolate press. The press changed how the treat could be made. Today, chocolate is common for many people around the world.

4

Utah

Utah was the 45th state to join the United States of America. It was a young state (only 24 years old) when Hal was born. There was still a great deal of farmland in Utah at this time.

A farmer works on his sugar beet farm in 1940.

Born to Fly

Gail Seymour Halvorsen was born in Salt Lake City, Utah, on October 10, 1920. Growing up, he worked on his family's sugar beet farm. But looking into the vast Utah sky, "Hal," as he was called, had another dream for his life. He wanted to fly.

In 1941, Hal earned his pilot's license. One day, Hal was flying over his family's farm. He started rolling his plane back and forth to "wave" to his parents. When he got home later that night, Hal found his father furious with him. His mother had seen Hal's plane rolling toward the ground. Hal's mother did not know the rolls were controlled, and she was upset. She thought her son was crashing! Hal's father told him to stop doing the rolls. Hal agreed. Instead, he learned to wave by simply wiggling his wings. He dipped them down, side to side. This experience would stick with Hal, and the wiggle would become Hal's **signature** move as a pilot.

Lindbergh

Earhart

Flying in the '40s

Hal was learning to fly about the time that famed pilots Charles Lindbergh and Amelia Earhart were in the news. Learning to fly was much rarer at that time than it is today. But even though technology has changed a great deal, the way in which planes fly is really the same today as it always was.

Now a pilot, Hal joined the Civil Air Patrol. World War II was in full swing when Japan bombed the U.S. **naval base** in Pearl Harbor, Hawai'i. That action prompted the United States to enter the war. Many young people, such as Hal, joined the **armed forces**. They wanted to help the war effort. Hal joined the U.S. Army Air Corps. There he trained as a fighter pilot. He then served as a transporter until the war ended. During that time, Hal's job was to fly people and equipment where they needed to go.

After the war, Hal stayed in the armed forces. In 1948, he was **stationed** in Alabama. It was there that he got orders to go to Germany. There was trouble between the Soviet Union and the rest of the Allies. Pilots were needed for an important mission. It was a matter of life and death for the people of Berlin.

Emergency responders race to the naval base moments after the attack on Pearl Harbor.

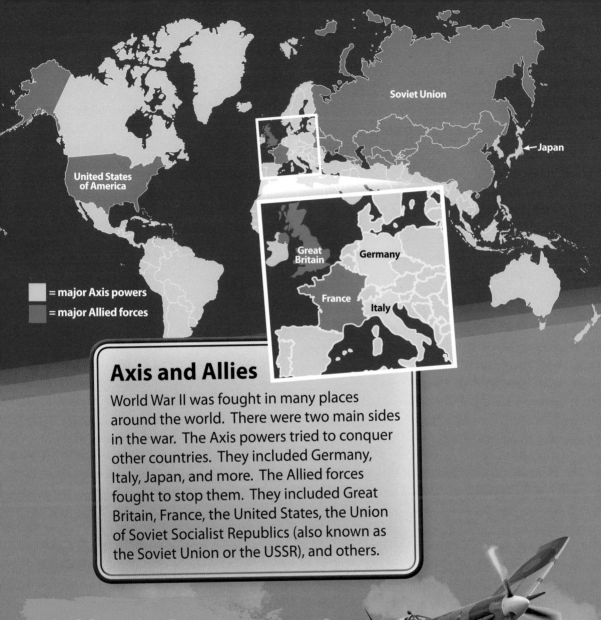

Soviet Union

Japan

United States
of America

Great
Britain

Germany

France

Italy

■ = major Axis powers
■ = major Allied forces

Axis and Allies

World War II was fought in many places around the world. There were two main sides in the war. The Axis powers tried to conquer other countries. They included Germany, Italy, Japan, and more. The Allied forces fought to stop them. They included Great Britain, France, the United States, the Union of Soviet Socialist Republics (also known as the Soviet Union or the USSR), and others.

Soldiers in the Air

There was no branch of the military that served in the air before the twentieth century. That is because air travel did not exist.

Spitfire planes were common in World War II.

Germany

Soviet
Zone

British
Zone

French
Zone

U.S. Zone

French
Zone

Berlin

French
Zone

British
Zone

Soviet
Zone

U.S. Zone

Berlin

The city of Berlin is nearly 800 years old. It marks its founding year as 1244, although it may have existed before that date. It was founded mainly because it was a good location for trade.

Berlin Divided

Pilots were needed for a special mission. They had to get food, medicine, and other goods to the people of West Berlin.

When World War II ended, the Allies **occupied** Germany. They split it into four zones. Great Britain, France, the United States, and the Soviet Union each took one zone. Berlin, the capital of Germany, was in the Soviet zone. But the other Allies wanted a piece of Berlin as well. It was a key spot for them all. So, the Soviet Union got East Berlin. The other three countries split up West Berlin.

At the start of the war, the Soviet Union supported the Axis side. Then, the Soviet Union joined the Allies during the war. But it was not a democracy, like other Allies were. The Soviet Union wanted Berlin to be **communist**. It wanted the people of Berlin to submit to their beliefs. The people refused. They did not want to give up their freedoms.

Communism

The theory behind communism is that everyone gets what they need. The government owns all property. Food and other goods are shared according to need. But communism in practice has often gone hand in hand with dictatorships. The people are not in charge. Those in power make the rules and may keep much of the country's wealth for themselves.

In 1948, the Allies created a new form of money for West Berlin. They were trying to help Germany recover from the war. But the Soviet Union thought the other Allied forces should have checked with them before doing this. They were angry. They said all other Allies had to leave Berlin. But the Allies would not leave. So, the Soviets set up a **blockade**. They would not let cars, trains, or boats get into West Berlin. Without transportation, food could not be delivered there. The Soviets thought the starving Berliners would force the Allies to leave. If they did, then food would be delivered again.

Berlin was in the Soviet zone of Germany. The Allies needed permission to get to West Berlin. Before the blockade, there was an unofficial agreement between the two sides that let the Allies pass through East Germany. But it was never written. What *was* written was that the Allied planes could fly into West Berlin. The Allies knew that the people of West Berlin needed help to get food. Pilots and planes could bring that help.

Behind the Blockade

The blockade was started by government leaders. But real people suffered while those leaders tried to gain control. People lost access to food and other resources. Families and friends on both sides of Berlin were separated from one another. To live behind a blockade is to live in a type of prison. The people were not free. Even so, despite their struggles, they were brave enough to resist Soviet control.

West Berliners watch East Berlin workers construct the Berlin Wall in 1961.

YOU ARE LEAVING
THE AMERICAN SECTOR
ВЫ ВЫЕЗЖАЕТЕ ИЗ
АМЕРИКАНСКОГО СЕКТОРА
VOUS SORTEZ
DU SECTEUR AMERICAIN

Berlin Wall

The Berlin Wall stood between East and West Berlin from 1961 to 1989. People from East Berlin were not allowed to go into West Berlin. Some families were divided on either side of the wall. The breaking down of the wall was a time of great celebration and, for many, marked the end of the **Cold War**.

Operation Vittles

At the time, there were about two million people in West Berlin. They were all in need of food, fuel, and other supplies. Providing for them became the work of the western Allies.

Within days of the Soviet Union announcing the blockade, there was a plan in place. The United States launched Operation Vittles. (*Vittles* is a slang word that means "food.") Great Britain launched its own plan—Operation Plainfare. Both countries' pilots began flying supplies into West Berlin.

Both missions ran around the clock. Planes took off from England and western Germany. As the blockade continued, more and more supplies were needed. At the height of the **airlift**, a plane was landing in West Berlin at least every 45 seconds. The cargo was quickly unloaded there. Then, the pilot flew away for more supplies. Pilots flew back and forth for 12 hours straight. Then, they went to sleep while the next crew took over.

Among these pilots was Hal. He worked hard, just as all the other pilots did. There was no time for anything, really, but work and sleep. But Hal had something more in mind.

Flying Boats

The British Royal Air Force used planes for their mission, but they also used flying boats. These were called Sunderlands. The Sunderlands were able to land on water.

Flights to Berlin

Soviet Zone

British Zone

French Zone

French Zone

U.S. Zone

Feeding the Masses

The Allies delivered around 6,000 tons of supplies each day. That is the same weight as 900 adult African elephants!

Hal wanted to see more of the city of Berlin. But there was no time between landing and taking off for a pilot to go anywhere. He decided to give up some of his rest time to explore and film the city. During his time off for sleep, Hal caught a ride into West Berlin on another pilot's plane. Once he landed, he went to take pictures of the planes landing while he waited for a car to pick him up.

It was this trip that changed things for Hal. He came upon a group of children standing along a fence. He was struck by their reaction to him. In other places around the world, children asked soldiers for candy and treats. These children asked for nothing. Hal wanted to give them something, but all he had were two sticks of gum. He broke the gum into pieces to share with those he could. Hal thought the children might fight over the gum. But, what happened next amazed Hal. The children passed around pieces of the wrappers so that everyone could smell their sweetness.

West Berliners watch a plane deliver food during the Berlin Airlift.

"Most Meaningful Lesson"

When Hal spoke with the children, he learned of their struggles during and since the war. But they told him that they knew they could survive the hunger as long as they were free. Hal said that the children taught him "the most meaningful lesson in freedom I've ever had."

Hal speaks to children through the fence.

Bits of Gum

The gum Hal offered the children was Wrigley's Doublemint®. This brand of gum was invented in 1914. It is still manufactured.

Enjoy Healthful Delicious
DOUBLEMINT GUM

WRIGLEY'S DOUBLEMINT CHEWING GUM

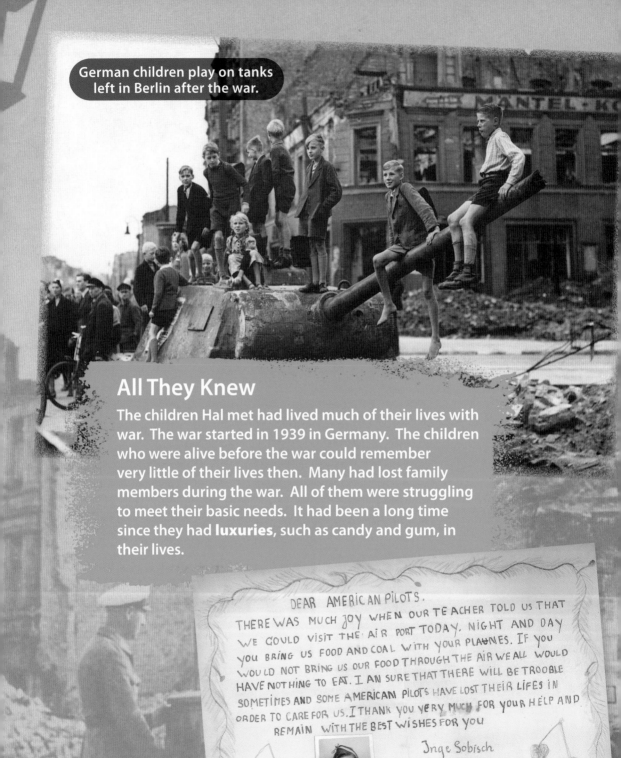

German children play on tanks left in Berlin after the war.

All They Knew

The children Hal met had lived much of their lives with war. The war started in 1939 in Germany. The children who were alive before the war could remember very little of their lives then. Many had lost family members during the war. All of them were struggling to meet their basic needs. It had been a long time since they had **luxuries**, such as candy and gum, in their lives.

DEAR AMERICAN PILOTS.

THERE WAS MUCH JOY WHEN OUR TEACHER TOLD US THAT WE COULD VISIT THE AIR PORT TODAY. NIGHT AND DAY YOU BRING US FOOD AND COAL WITH YOUR PLAUNES. IF YOU WOULD NOT BRING US OUR FOOD THROUGH THE AIR WE ALL WOULD HAVE NOTHING TO EAT. I AN SURE THAT THERE WILL BE TROOBLE SOMETIMES AND SOME AMERICAN PILOTS HAVE LOST THEIR LIFES IN ORDER TO CARE FOR US. I THANK YOU VERY MUCH FOR YOUR HELP AND REMAIN WITH THE BEST WISHES FOR YOU

Inge Sobisch

Berlin-Schöneberg
Naumannstraße 7.

Operation Little Vittles

As Hal left the children, a landing plane caught his attention. It gave him a bold new idea! Why not drop enough gum and candy for all the children from his plane? He excitedly told them his plan. They had to agree to share the treats with one another. If they agreed, Hal would drop treats the next day, and the children could gather there to pick them up.

The children were excited, but they wondered how they would recognize his plane. So many planes flew overhead, and they could not tell who flew which plane. Then, Hal remembered his old flying trick from back home. He told the children that he would wiggle his wings when nearing the spot. His plane would wave to the children just as he had made it wave to his parents on their farm in Utah. Hal had to explain what a *wiggle* was since the children's English was **limited**. But once they understood, they could not wait to watch for his wiggling wings!

Language Learners

English was not commonly taught in Germany before World War II. There were four children in the group who spoke to Hal in English. They told Hal how the war had changed their lives.

Hal caught a flight back to his base in western Germany, where he quickly realized how tricky his plan would be. He did not have enough candy for all the children, and he would have to find a way to get more. He also did not have the permission of his **commanders**. In the armed forces, it is not okay to act without their knowledge and permission. But Hal figured this was a one-time deal, and he also knew it would make a huge difference for the children. He quickly came up with a plan.

Hal found a way to use **rations** to get the candy. The next challenge was to figure out how to drop the treats. A dropped package would be heavy and fall to the ground too quickly. The weight and speed could be dangerous to anyone below. Then, Hal thought of parachutes. Parachutes would slow the descent and let the packages land softly. Hal made tiny parachutes from three **handkerchiefs**. He tied the candy to them—and hoped it would work!

Rations to Spare

Pilots received **ration cards**, but Hal only had enough rations to purchase a little chocolate and gum at a time. It would not be enough for all the children. Hal knew he needed the help of his fellow pilots. He asked if they would share their rations so he would have enough for the kids. Without hesitating, they did.

Tough Landings

Hal was based out of an airport in West Germany. It was very difficult to land a plane there. For one **runway**, pilots had to fly between apartment buildings before landing. For another runway, pilots had fly over a building before diving their planes to the ground!

The next day, Hal wiggled his wings and gave a signal to his **crew chief**, Sergeant Herschel Elkins. The sergeant dropped the parachutes from emergency **flare** tubes. Then, they both hoped the parachutes found their target!

Hal landed and his plane was quickly unloaded. Once back in the air, it did not take long to see that the treats had reached the children. He saw the kids waving his handkerchiefs at all the pilots in the air. They knew that one of the pilots must be Uncle Wiggly Wings.

Hal was so pleased with the efforts that he made two more drops to growing numbers of children. But his good works could not stay a secret for long. Very soon, big stacks of letters started arriving at the airport. The letters were addressed to *The Chocolate Pilot* or to *Uncle Wiggly Wings*.

Hal made one last drop—or so he thought. The next day, he was called to his commander's office. He was sure he was in some big trouble.

Hal shows how his crew chief dropped parachutes out of the flare tube.

Uncle Wiggly Wings

This was the pet name the children of Berlin gave Hal. *Uncle* showed the warmth with which they regarded him. He was like a dear uncle to them. His wiggly wings made them laugh and cheer. He brought great hope and joy to the children of Berlin.

In the News

A newspaper reporter happened to be near a candy drop and was almost hit in the head. He wrote about the parachutes. Hal's boss saw the paper, which included a photo of his plane with its identifying number visible on the tail. The secret was out!

WIESBADEN, Germany, Oct. 14 (Reuters)—Thousands of German and refugee children in west Germany are looking forward eagerly to being "bombed" by a four-motored American plane next week.

The missiles, candy and chocolate bars, will be dropped on tiny parachutes during the final mission of the little vittles candy operation. This was begun on July 20 by Lt. Gale S. Halverson, 27, Garland, Utah, when he was an air lift pilot.

A U.S. Army Air Forces general had seen a newspaper article and called Hal's commander. The commander wasted no time in talking to Hal. But what he said was a surprise. The Air Forces liked what Hal was doing! The reporter in the newspaper had called the candy drop "Operation Little Vittles." The Air Forces wanted to make it a true operation. Word spread that supplies were needed. People from around the world began to send what they could. Candy companies did too. In fact, they sent tons and tons of candy.

Readers to the Rescue!

Weekly Reader was a news magazine written for children. They wrote an article about Operation Little Vittles. Pretty soon, children around the world started sending in their own gum and candy. They read about the mission and wanted to help.

Hal started to print "please return" on the parachutes so they could be reused. The children did return most of them. The children also sent parachutes they had made with thank you notes. They were deeply grateful to Hal and all the pilots. Operation Vittles was food for their bodies. But Operation Little Vittles was food for their hearts and souls.

Helping Pete

A nine-year-old boy named Pete Zimmerman wrote to Hal to say big kids were getting all the candy. He drew Hal a map to drop candy at Pete's house! Hal tried but it did not work. So, Hal mailed candy to Pete instead. Pete told Hal that his parents had died in the war and that he wanted to live in the United States. Pete was later adopted and grew up in Pennsylvania. He wrote letters to Hal for many years.

Hal tosses extra parachutes to the waiting children at Tempelhof.

LAND OF CHRISTMAS

19TH TROOP

Commander

Twenty-four years after the airlift, Hal was named commander of the air base at Tempelhof Central Airport. This was the site of Operation Little Vittles.

Life of Service

Since that time all those years ago, Hal has lived a life of service. He married and had a family, and he was promoted to the rank of colonel. Hal has returned to Berlin many times. The children he helped still speak of him with great love and gratitude. Many have tears in their eyes when they talk about him.

The Berlin blockade lasted for 11 months. More than 250,000 flights were made. Hal says that when times are tough, it is more important than ever to serve others. He is grateful to have been a part of the operations. He says that "fulfillment in life comes from service." And he is quick to add that great rewards come to those who serve. Surely, his life has proven this. In Berlin, Hal often stays with the children—who are now parents and grandparents— he helped all those years ago. He is still their Uncle Wiggly Wings. For Hal, there is no greater praise. And he is grateful.

New School

The people of Frankfurt, Germany, named a school for Hal. It is the Gail S. Halverson Elementary School. The school is on an air base.

Make It!

Hal had to find a way to make parachutes from handkerchiefs. He also had to attach candy bars and gum to the parachutes so they would stay together when dropped from airplanes.

Be like Hal! Make candy parachutes from fabric and string. Follow these steps:

1. Take a handkerchief, bandana, or other lightweight square of strong fabric. Also get strong string, chocolate candy bars, and gum.

2. Use the fabric and string to make a small parachute.

3. Try dropping the candy parachute from a high place (such as the top of a stairwell). Be sure you are safe and in no danger of falling! Also, be sure there is no one to get hurt below.

4. Does your candy make it safely to the ground? If not, try a new way to make your parachute.

Glossary

airlift—an event in which things or people are carried by airplanes when other methods are not possible

armed forces—the military organizations of a country

blockade—a system by which one group stops people or supplies from entering or leaving an area

Cold War—a time in the 20th century in which there was opposition between the United States and the Soviet Union

commanders—people in charge of military forces

communist—run by a government that owns all property and that gives people goods according to their needs

crew chief—an aircraft maintenance chief in the military

flare—refers to a very bright light that can be used as a signal or to light up something

handkerchiefs—squares of cloth that a person uses for hygiene, such as blowing one's nose

limited—not at its full potential

luxuries—rare treats that can be expensive or hard to get

naval base—a place where a country's navy keeps supplies and where people work

occupied—used soldiers to control a foreign country

ration cards—official documents that are used to keep track of or purchase a person's allowed rations

rations—amounts of food or supplies that governments allow people to have

runway—a piece of land where planes take off and land

signature—something that someone or something is known for

stationed—assigned to live and work in an area while doing a job or waiting for a task

wafted—drifted slowly through the air